WHY SHOULD I EAT THIS CARROT?

✦ and other questions about healthy eating ✦

Louise Spilsbury

www.heinemann.co.uk/library
Visit our website to find out more information about **Heinemann Library** books.

To order:
☎ Phone 44 (0) 1865 888066
📄 Send a fax to 44 (0) 1865 314091
💻 Visit the Heinemann Bookshop at www.heinemann.co.uk/library to browse our catalogue and order online.

First published in Great Britain by Heinemann Library, Halley Court, Jordan Hill, Oxford OX2 8EJ, part of Harcourt Education. Heinemann is a registered trademark of Harcourt Education Ltd.

Editorial: Nancy Dickmann, Jennifer Tubbs and Louise Galpine
Design: David Poole and Tokay Interactive Ltd (www.tokay.co.uk)
Illustrations: Kamae Design Ltd
Picture Research: Rebecca Sodergren and Liz Eddison
Production: Séverine Ribierre and Jonathan Smith

Originated by Ambassador Litho Ltd
Printed in China by Wing King Tong

ISBN 0 431 11090 5
07 06 05 04 03
10 9 8 7 6 5 4 3 2 1

British Library Cataloguing in Publication Data
Spilsbury, Louise
Why Should I Eat this Carrot? and other questions about healthy eating
613.2
A full catalogue record for this book is available from the British Library.

Acknowledgements
Chris Honeywell p. **20**; Corbis pp. **6** (Dennis M Gottlieb) **9** (Lynda Richardson), **10** (Tom Stewart), **11** (S Carmona), **13** (Peter Beck), **17** (Laura Dwight), **21** (Reed Kaestner), **28** (Charles Gupton); Getty Images pp. **4**, **12**, **18**, **22** (Taxi), **5**, **8** (Stone); Liz Eddison p. **26**; Photodisc p. **14**; Trevor Clifford pp. **15**, **16**, **19**, **24**; Tudor Photography pp. **23**, **25**, **27**.

Cover photograph of child eating carrot, reproduced with permission of Tudor Photography.

The publishers would like to thank Julie Johnson for her assistance in the preparation of this book.

Every effort has been made to contact copyright holders of any material reproduced in this book. Any omissions will be rectified in subsequent printings if notice is given to the publishers.

CONTENTS

Words appearing in the text in bold, **like this**, are explained in the Glossary.

WHY IS HEALTHY EATING IMPORTANT?

You may have heard the old saying 'You are what you eat'. This may sound like nonsense, but it is true. The food you eat provides your body with the **energy** it needs to live, and with the materials it needs to grow and to repair parts that are worn out or damaged.

Staying alive

Our bodies are made up of millions of tiny **cells**. These are so small that you can only see them through a microscope. Up to when you are about eighteen years old, your body makes new cells, so that you can grow. When you are an adult, your body continues to make new cells to replace old or damaged ones. The energy to make and to repair body cells comes from the food you eat. To build a strong and healthy body, you need to eat healthy kinds of food.

You need energy for everything you do – from sleeping to skateboarding.

What are nutrients?

The parts of food your body uses for growth and energy are called **nutrients**. You cannot see or taste them, but you need a variety of nutrients for your body to work properly and to stay healthy. There are five main kinds of nutrients — **proteins**, **fats**, **minerals**, **vitamins** and **carbohydrates**. To be healthy, you also need to drink water and eat **fibre**. You will find out more about all of these types of nutrients in this book.

We need to eat a healthy mixture of different foods, because different nutrients help your body in different ways.

WHAT IS A DIET?

When you hear people say that they are on a diet, what they really mean is that they are on a slimming diet, to lose weight. In fact, your diet is basically the food you eat every day. A balanced diet means eating the foods that make your body healthy.

5

HOW DOES MY BODY TURN FOOD INTO ENERGY?

Food contains all the **nutrients** your body needs to live and grow, but digestion is needed to break food into separate bits that your body can use.

The food on your plate is no good to your body as it is. So that it can use food, your body has to break it down into pieces so tiny they can get into your blood. This process is called **digestion**.

Digesting food

Your body starts to digest food as soon as you put it into your mouth. Your teeth chew and bite the food into smaller pieces, and mix it with saliva (spit) to make it soft. Then your tongue pushes the mashed-up food into your throat so that you can swallow it. **Muscles** inside the oesophagus – a long tube leading down from your throat – move the food down to your stomach.

Food stays in your stomach for about five hours. Here, special juices break the bits of food into even smaller pieces. When these move into the small intestine, they are mixed with more digestive juices until they become so small that they can pass into your blood.

Nutrients in the blood

Your blood is like a fleet of delivery trucks that travels around your body through a network of tubes called blood vessels. Your blood drops off nutrients from the digested food to the different kinds of **cells** all over your body. The cells use this **energy** to divide and increase in number so that you can grow, and also to repair themselves when they are damaged.

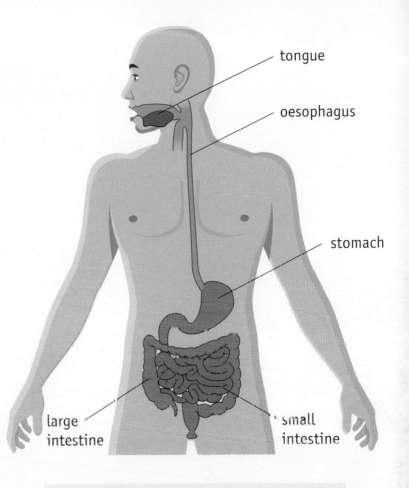

tongue

oesophagus

stomach

large intestine

small intestine

Food takes about a day to pass through your whole **digestive system**. Unwanted bits move from the small intestine to the large intestine. This waste passes out of your body when you go to the toilet.

WHY SHOULD I DRINK WATER?

Water is the most important **nutrient** of all. Your body can survive for weeks without food, but only a few days without water. In fact, you are made up mostly of water! Your body can only work properly if you keep your water levels up.

Water in your body

All of the fluids in your body contain water. Some of these, such as blood, are your body's transport system, carrying nutrients and **oxygen** to parts that need them, and taking away waste. Water keeps parts, such as **joints**, lubricated (moving freely). Watery saliva moves food through your **digestive system**. Water also forms a cushion over important parts, such as your brain, to protect them from knocks.

If you are too hot, you sweat. Sweat is mostly water and, as it dries off your skin, it takes heat with it and cools you down. When you sweat, you need to drink more to replace this water.

Topping up your water

You lose lots of water every day – through sweat, urination (wee) and other things your body does – and you need to top yourself up again. You should drink about six glasses of water a day, but you can get some of this water from foods that contain lots of water, such as fruit, vegetables and soup. You cannot substitute other drinks, such as fizzy drinks, for water. Pure water is the best possible drink.

Nine-tenths of the weight of some fruit and vegetables, such as melon or cucumber, is water.

WHAT IS DEHYDRATION?

Dehydration is when your body has lost more water than it has taken in. Sometimes, people get dehydrated when they are sick, or because they do not drink enough water when it is hot and they are sweating. It is very unhealthy to get dehydrated, so drink water often – don't wait until you feel thirsty.

9

WHY DO ATHLETES EAT PASTA?

Some athletes eat pasta, and foods such as bread, cereals, rice and potatoes, when they are training, because these foods give them **energy**. They are called **carbohydrates**. Most people do not need to eat lots of carbohydrates before a race or match, but you should always try to make carbohydrates the main part of every meal.

Carbohydrates for energy

When you **digest** your food, most of it is broken down into glucose, a kind of sugar. The glucose moves into your blood. The blood carries the glucose and **oxygen** (a gas from the air that we breathe in) all over your body. The glucose and oxygen are mixed inside the body's **cells** and, when they react together, they release energy.

Carbohydrates are the body's fuel – they are **nutrients** that give you the energy you need to beat your friend at chess or to ride your bike.

Energy for later

Some of the glucose that your body does not use right away is stored in cells in your **liver** and **muscles**, in a form called glycogen. If there is too much glycogen to store in your liver and muscle cells, the rest is stored as body fat.

Later on, your body can use these glycogen stores for energy, just as a car uses petrol from its fuel tank. If you do a short burst of exercise, such as running for a bus, your body uses the glycogen for energy. If you do a lot of exercise for longer, perhaps when you play in a football match or take the dog for a walk, your body uses up some of your fat store for energy.

Marathon runners have to race 26 miles (nearly 42 kilometres) without a lunch break, so they know how important carbohydrates are for giving you energy that lasts.

Kinds of carbohydrates

There are two kinds of **carbohydrates** – simple and complex. Simple carbohydrates are those that your body can digest and absorb into the blood, simply and quickly. Sugar is a simple carbohydrate, and you find it in cakes, sweets and other sweet foods. Many fruits contain a kind of sugar, too. Fruits are a lot better for you because they also contain other healthy **nutrients**.

Complex carbohydrates take longer to travel through your body's **digestive system** – they are more complex, and trickier to digest. Because of this, they release **energy** more slowly and over a longer period of time. You find complex carbohydrates – sometimes called starchy foods – in bread, cereals, rice, pasta, noodles, potatoes and many other varieties of vegetables.

Complex carbohydrates, such as pasta, are better for you than simple carbohydrates. As well as giving you lots of slow-release energy, they also contain **fat** and **fibre**, to help you to be healthy.

Staple foods

Staple foods are those that people eat a lot of because they grow well in their country. For example, in China rice is a staple food. Staple foods are always carbohydrates, and they are called staple – meaning basic and necessary – because people need them to live. Even if you eat a variety of carbohydrates, you should try to make them a staple part of your diet, by eating some at every meal and also as snacks sometimes.

In Central America, maize (corn) is a staple food, because it is the main carbohydrate that people eat.

WHAT ARE CALORIES?

Calories are a measure of how much energy a food can supply your body with. At your age, you need about 2400 calories every day, because your body uses up a lot of energy to keep you going and growing. Carbohydrates contain useful calories – two slices of bread or one banana each give you about 100 calories.

13

WHY IS BROWN BREAD BETTER THAN WHITE?

Bread is made using flour, and flour is made from crushed grains (seeds) of wheat. White flour is made from the inside of the grain. Wholemeal flour is made from the whole grain, including the skin around the seed, called bran. Brown – wholemeal – bread is good for you, because bran contains **fibre**, which helps to keep your body healthy.

Lots of fibre

All plant foods contain fibre – little thin strands like threads. You can see them easily in plant foods, such as celery. The problem is that many of the foods we eat are processed – they are treated and changed to make the food products you see in packets and tins. Processing often removes the fibre so, to be healthy, you should eat more fresh fruit and vegetables. Aim to eat five pieces every day.

To make white bread, the bran is removed from the seeds that grow on wheat plants like these. Brown bread still has this nutritious outer layer.

Fibre for health

Fibre is not a **nutrient**. In fact, it is a part of food that we cannot **digest** at all but, as it passes through our bodies, it helps our **digestive system** to work properly. Fibre soaks up water like a sponge, making waste material from your food softer. This means that it passes through the large intestine and out of your body more quickly. This is good, because it is unhealthy to have food waste in your body for too long.

SOME FIBRE-RICH FOODS

These foods contain lots of fibre:

- fresh and dried fruit, such as bananas and apricots
- porridge
- vegetables, such as broccoli and potatoes
- beans, such as baked beans
- nuts and seeds, such as sunflower seeds and peanuts.

This picture shows you some of the foods that contain fibre. Fibre-rich foods stop you getting constipation – when your faeces (poo) become too dry and hard to pass easily out of your body.

15

ARE SMOOTHIES GOOD FOR YOU?

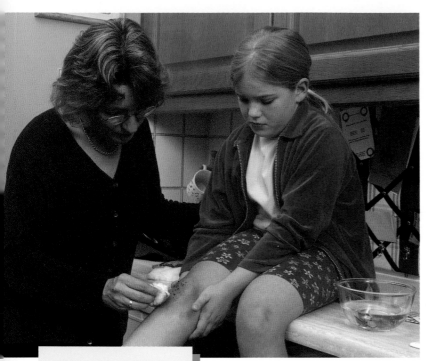

When you fall and hurt yourself, it is protein that helps your cuts and grazes to heal.

Smoothies, or milkshakes, are good for you – not just because they can taste so good, but because they are great sources of **protein**. Milk and other dairy products, such as cheese, are rich in protein, and protein is a very important **nutrient** that everyone needs to build a healthy body.

Protein – the body builder

Protein is often called the body builder, because it is the main ingredient in all of your body parts, including your **muscles**, skin and **liver**. You also need protein to replace or to repair parts when they are worn out or damaged, and to make haemoglobin, the part of your blood that carries vital **oxygen** around your body. Protein has another important job. It makes antibodies, which are special **cells** that attack **infections** and diseases that can make you ill.

What is protein?

Protein is not just a single substance – it is made up of many smaller parts, called amino acids. When you **digest** protein foods, your body breaks them down into these separate parts. Then your body uses the different amino acids like building blocks. It puts them together again, in different combinations, to build the many cells that form the different parts of your body.

Your body can make some of the amino acids you need by using substances that are already stored inside your body. The other amino acids that you need – called essential amino acids – can only get into your body from protein foods. Because of this, it is very important to eat some protein foods every day.

Your body uses protein to build body parts, but whether it makes healthy hair or strong fingers depends on which amino acids – the building blocks of protein – it contains.

WHAT IF I AM A VEGETARIAN?

If you are a vegetarian, you do not eat meat – so how do you get all the protein you need when plant foods do not contain all the essential amino acids? Different kinds of plant foods have different amino acids, so the trick is to mix them together to be healthy.

Protein foods

There is some **protein** in all foods. Animal foods that are rich in protein include meat and fish, and dairy products, such as cheese. Plant foods that contain protein include beans, lentils, nuts and grains (seeds). Animal proteins contain almost all of the essential amino acids a body needs. Many plant foods, however, are low on or lack certain essential amino acids.

If you are a vegetarian, it is easy to mix different proteins. When you eat pizza you are combining grains and a dairy product.

How much protein should I eat?

Although proteins are vitally important to your health, you do not need to eat a huge amount of them. In fact, many protein foods also contain **fats**, so it is unhealthy to eat more than you need. If you eat a protein food, or a mix of protein foods, as part of your main meals twice a day, and perhaps include them in your snacks sometimes, you should get all you need.

The important thing is to eat some foods with protein in them every day. Your body cannot store proteins, so you need to keep topping yourself up with these **nutrients**.

When choosing protein foods, do not just think about how much protein they have. Peanut butter is a good protein choice, but it is less healthy for you if it has lots of added sugar and salt.

WHY SHOULD I EAT THIS CARROT?

If you want to watch fireworks at night, or enjoy a rainbow, eat your carrots! Carrots contain **vitamin** A – a **nutrient** that helps your eyes to see well in the dark and to tell the difference between colours. Vitamin A is just one of the vitamins your body needs to be healthy.

Different kinds of vitamins

There are two kinds of vitamins – fat-soluble and water-soluble. Vitamins A, D, E and K are fat-soluble, because your body stores them in body fat (and in your **liver**). Vitamin C and the different B vitamins are water-soluble, because they become part of the water that makes up your blood. If they are not used up as they travel round your body with your blood, they pass out of it when you urinate (wee).

We have to get the vitamins we need from our food. You need to eat food that contains water-soluble vitamins, such as oranges, every day, because your body cannot store them.

VITAL VITAMINS

This list tells you the main vitamins you need, how they help you and where to find them.

vitamin A   Helps with eyesight, growth and healthy skin. Found in fruits, vegetables and milk.

B vitamins   Help you to make **energy** and healthy blood **cells**. Found in fish, meats, eggs, beans, bread ... egetables.

... you healthy gums and teeth, ... **muscles** and bones, and ... you to fight **infections** and ... wounds. Found in fruits and ... vegetables.

... to build strong bones and ... and helps you to absorb a ... called **calcium**. Found in ... ish, eggs and nuts.

... ts your body's **tissues**, and ... you to use other vitamins ... ly. Found in vegetable oils, ... vegetables and nuts.

... your blood to clot when you are cut. Found in dark green vegetables and cheese.

What are minerals?

You often hear **vitamins** linked with another **nutrient** – **minerals**. Like vitamins, minerals are vital for your health, and you only need small amounts of them. Two important minerals are **calcium** and iron.

Calcium

Calcium is especially important for building strong bones and teeth. It also helps your **muscles** and nerves to work properly. You get the calcium you need from milk and other dairy products, such as yoghurt and cheese, and from leafy green vegetables, such as cabbage.

If you get low on iron, you feel tired and lacking in **energy**. When people do not have enough iron for a long time, they get an illness called **anaemia**.

Iron

Your body needs iron to help your blood to carry the **oxygen** that you breathe in around your body. Your body parts need oxygen to make energy from your food. Meats, fish, raisins and cereals are good sources of iron.

Other minerals

Your body needs tiny amounts of many different minerals with interesting-sounding names, such as zinc, magnesium and phosphorus. You often see these listed on food packets. Don't worry – you do not have to read lots of labels to check that you are getting all the minerals you need – just eat a healthy diet with different kinds of food.

Salt is another important mineral, but you should get enough from your food. Too much salt is bad for you, so there is no need to add extra to your food.

DO I NEED VITAMIN AND MINERAL PILLS?

If you eat a wide range of foods, you get all the vitamins and minerals you need. Many people who take pills with extra nutrients – called supplements – probably do not need them, but it should not do them any harm, because the body just excretes (gets rid of) any it does not use.

WHAT IS SO BAD ABOUT FAT?

People are warned not to eat too many fatty foods because they contain a lot of **calories**. Your body can only use so many calories at a time, so it stores the rest as body fat. This makes some people overweight. Overweight people are more likely to suffer from health problems when they are older, such as heart disease and **diabetes**.

Is some fat good for me?

It is vital for your body to have some fatty foods. Your body uses **fat** to give you **energy**, and many of your body **cells** need fats to form properly. Having a thin layer of fat around you keeps your body warm and cushions your insides from bumps.

No food type is really bad for you – what counts is how often you eat it and what else you eat. Some fats, such as butter, are fine in small amounts, and even contain some healthy **vitamins**.

Which foods contain fat?

There are two main kinds of fat — saturated and unsaturated. Saturated fats are found in red meats and dairy products. Unsaturated fats are found in fish and white meats, such as chicken, and in plant parts or products, such as avocados and olive oil. Unsaturated fats are slightly healthier than saturated fats, but you should not eat too much of either.

FAT-BUSTING TIPS

Here are some ways you can avoid eating too much fat:

- eat grilled, steamed, microwaved or stir-fried food, instead of food that has been roasted or fried in lots of oil
- eat yoghurt with your fruit or puddings, instead of cream
- eat baked potatoes rather than chips
- eat fish or chicken instead of beef, sometimes.

This girl is tucking into a salmon and cream cheese bagel. The fat in oily fish, such as salmon, is good for you. It helps your blood to flow around your body more easily.

25

WHY WASH FRUIT BEFORE EATING IT?

Washing or scrubbing fruits and vegetables well before you eat them is better than peeling, because the most nutritious part is just below the surface of their skins!

Many farms use artificial chemicals to help crops to grow bigger. They also use chemicals to kill pests that try to eat food plants while they are growing. Often, these chemicals stay on the skin of fruits and vegetables when they get to the shops. That is why it is best to wash or peel fresh foods – to get rid of any chemicals before you eat them.

What are organic foods?

Organic farms grow crops and raise animals without using artificial chemicals. Instead, farmers use compost and manure from farm animals to feed the land, and other plants and insects to control pests. Some people believe that organic food is safer to eat than food that is grown using chemicals.

26

Always keep pets and flies away from food, because they can spread germs.

Keeping food clean and fresh

You need to eat food that is clean and fresh, or it can make you ill. Wash your hands before eating or preparing food, to stop germs getting on to your food. Store food properly, according to the instructions on labels. **Bacteria** from raw foods, such as meat, spread to cooked foods easily, so keep them apart in the fridge. Don't eat food that has gone bad, because this means that bacteria are growing on it, and some bacteria can make you ill.

WHAT ARE GM FOODS?

GM stands for 'genetically modified'. GM foods come from plants that scientists have changed by adding or taking away certain **genes**. Some people avoid GM foods, because they are not sure what effects these changes to the plants could have on our health.

WHAT MAKES A HEALTHY SNACK?

IDEAS FOR HEALTHY SNACKS

Why not try pretzels, unbuttered popcorn, fruit, fruit smoothies, breadsticks, crackers, bagels, rice cakes, fruit or cereal bars, sticks of carrot, celery or pepper or a bowl of wholewheat cereal without added sugar?

Your body is growing fast, and it is natural to want a snack sometimes. The body can use sweet and fatty foods, such as biscuits and crisps, to make **energy** quickly, but the energy only lasts a short time. Also, these foods have few **nutrients**. Starchy **carbohydrates**, such as cereals or bread, take longer to **digest** and give you energy for longer. These and other healthy snacks, such as fruit, also give your body some of the **vitamins**, **minerals** and **fibre** it needs.

It is fine to eat sweet or fatty snacks sometimes, but try to eat healthy snacks more often.

28

HEALTHY EATING

This food plate is an easy way to see the variety of foods that make a healthy diet, and the kind of amounts of them you should eat.

GLOSSARY

anaemia illness that makes you feel weak and tired. It is caused by a lack of iron in the blood.

bacteria tiny living things that can cause disease

calcium mineral that your body needs for strong bones and teeth

calories measure of the energy value of food

carbohydrates kinds of food that give you energy

cells smallest building block of living things

diabetes people who have diabetes are unable to use food to make the energy their body needs

digest/digestion way the body breaks down the food we eat

digestive system parts of the body that digest food

energy energy allows living things to do everything they need to live and grow

fats types of food that are naturally oily or greasy

fibre parts of plant foods, such as vegetables and fruit, which the body cannot digest

genes information in all living things that determines the way they are

infection kind of disease that can be caught by other people

joint   place where two bones join

liver   organ in the body that stores nutrients from the blood and breaks down waste

minerals   chemicals found in rocks and soil

muscles   bunches of fibres that move the different parts of your body

nutrients   kinds of chemicals found in food that we need to be healthy

oxygen   gas in the air around us

proteins   substances in some of the foods we eat that our bodies can use to build or repair body parts

tissues   groups of cells connected together

vitamins   nutrients your body needs

FURTHER READING

Why Do I Vomit? And Other Questions About Digestion, Angela Royston (Heinemann Library, 2002)

Staying Healthy: Eating Right, Alice B. McGinty (Power Kids Press, 1999)

The Children's Step-by-Step Cookbook, Angela Wilkes (Dorling Kindersley, 1994)

INDEX